A COMPREHENSIVE GUIDE FOR AUTHORS

A COMPREHENSIVE GUIDE FOR AUTHORS

SLOANE MONTGOMERY

CONTENTS

Introduction to the Writing Process   1

1 Crafting Your Manuscript   4

2 Editing and Revising Your Work   7

3 Preparing for Publication   10

4 Navigating the Publishing Industry   14

5 Building Your Author Platform   17

6 Marketing and Promoting Your Book   20

7 Engaging with Readers   23

8 Copyright and Legal Considerations   26

9 Achieving Success as an Author   29

Conclusion and Next Steps   32

Copyright © 2025 by Sloane Montgomery
All rights reserved. No part of this book may be reproduced in any manner whatsoever without written permission except in the case of brief quotations embodied in critical articles and reviews.
First Printing, 2025

Introduction to the Writing Process

Publication can be an immensely rewarding endeavor, but it requires significant effort and meticulous preparation. Some researchers have a natural aptitude for writing and can effectively expand upon even the simplest of ideas. Others, however, may need focused practice to hone these skills. Regardless of where one begins, every seasoned researcher must undertake writing as an essential practice—not only to articulate their own ideas but also to mentor and develop the skills of their colleagues and staff.

Writing and publication serve as more than mere personal achievements; they act as a tangible measure of professional growth and success. The number of publications attributed to a researcher often correlates with their career trajectory. In many organizations, publications are highly valued, viewed as both an indicator of expertise and a pathway to recognition. Researchers who contribute meaningfully to the advancement of knowledge within their field often earn professional rewards, including promotions and increased opportunities for collaboration.

To embark on a journey as an author or publisher of scientific works is to enter a realm dedicated to the art of the written word. This field draws from the wisdom of philosophers, poets, historians, novelists, and even journalists, merging their insights with rigorous scientific inquiry. While it is impossible for a book like this to encompass the entirety of knowledge about authorship and publication, it aims to provide practical guidance to improve your craft as a writer and researcher.

Today's researchers face an overabundance of publications, leaving many feeling overwhelmed. In this age of information, the pressing question becomes: *Why should one choose to write this particular manuscript?* The answer lies in the unique contribution you, as an author, can make to the ongoing dialogue in your field.

Understanding the Creative Process

At the heart of scientific writing lies creativity—a process fueled by imagination, intuition, and instinct. Imagination enables the creation of associative imagery, linking seemingly unrelated ideas. Intuition allows for leaps of understanding, forming connections that bridge the known with the unknown. Instinct, meanwhile, serves as an innate guide, shaping behaviors and decisions. Together, these qualities form the intellectual and emotional vision necessary for innovative research.

To possess such vision is to embody the spirit of scientific discovery. It empowers researchers to perceive what is needed for confirmation, transforming raw ideas into meaningful insights. Intuition, vision, and inspiration are not separate forces; they are intertwined, each one enhancing the other in the pursuit of knowledge.

The decision to initiate a research study—and to ultimately publish its findings—is an intentional act of exploration. It signifies a deliberate commitment to contribute to humanity's scientific awareness. Engaging in this process means navigating uncharted territory and embracing the challenges of productivity.

While inspiration can often be sparked by encounters with the work of others, it is not always a guarantee. There are times when the absence of connection with another's writing can lead to feelings of dissatisfaction or disillusionment. However, it is essential to remember that creative breakthroughs are often the result of perseverance rather than flashes of brilliance. Some of the most impactful scientific contributions have emerged from sustained effort and unwavering determination.

An imaginative mind has the ability to sift through complexities, identify key insights, and build bridges between disparate ideas. By pressing forward, even in the absence of immediate inspiration, researchers can transform obstacles into opportunities and bring their creative visions to life.

CHAPTER 1

Crafting Your Manuscript

Writing is both an art and a demanding craft. It's a process that requires discipline, determination, and dedication—just ask any professional writer. While this manual is designed to guide you through the journey of authorship, it cannot replace your responsibility to communicate your research in clear, concise, and impactful language. As seasoned writers and editors can attest, there's no substitute for the hard work of drafting, revising, and meticulously editing your text, whether it's a novel, research article, business plan, biography, or any other type of writing.

A polished and well-structured manuscript not only captivates your audience but also conveys your message with ease and precision. Such texts are more enjoyable to read, more likely to be remembered, and—crucially—more influential. Effective research communication often has one key goal: to inspire and persuade. Achieving this involves presenting data and ideas dynamically. Instead of overwhelming your readers with endless paragraphs of dry text, consider incorporating vibrant figures, tables, and illustrations. These visual elements can stand as their own analyses, reducing word count while igniting interest and enhancing understanding.

Consistency is equally important. Strive for a uniform paper structure across all sections—whether you're presenting your argument, describing your methods, reporting results, or drawing conclusions. Remember, not all sections of your manuscript carry equal weight. Be prepared to trim substantial portions of your initial drafts to sharpen your narrative. Focus on *writing something* rather than trying to perfect your draft from the outset; even bad drafts, rough memos, or unpolished emails are essential steps in the process. Writing well begins with writing often.

A Winning Style, Language, and Structure

To craft a compelling research paper, focus on a cohesive style, thoughtful language, and a clear structure. Begin with a well-organized abstract—this is often the gateway to your work. Ensure your titles and subtitles are concise and informative, capturing the essence of your paper while engaging the reader. Divide your manuscript into distinct sections with meaningful subheadings, which help to maintain readability and structure.

Editing is as much an art as writing itself. Use each revision to refine grammar, punctuation, and spelling. A winning manuscript balances technical accuracy with a narrative style that draws the reader in. Consider developing a style guide for longer projects to ensure consistency across various sections and among team members involved in writing or publishing.

Developing Characters and Plot

If your manuscript involves storytelling—whether fictional or narrative-based research—developing relatable characters and a compelling plot is vital. A character who is perpetually victimized without striving to improve their circumstances may alienate readers. Sympathetic characters are those who grow and evolve, creating an emotional connection with the audience.

Character development begins with intentionality. Build rich, multi-dimensional characters by exploring their personalities, habits, hobbies, occupations, and lifestyles. What is their personal history? What motivates them? Beyond these external traits, delve into their inner lives: their primary goals, subconscious needs, and areas for growth. Inner conflicts and moments of realization bring authenticity and depth to your characters, making them resonate with readers.

How to Write an Outline

An outline is the backbone of any manuscript. It provides structure and direction, transforming a chaotic collection of ideas into a cohesive narrative. The process begins with organizing your research notes—breaking them down, categorizing them, and summarizing key points.

Once you have compiled your notes, the challenge lies in constructing a workable outline. This task can feel daunting, especially when you hit a creative block midway through the process. However, even a half-finished outline is a step forward, providing a foundation to build upon. If your writing flow is interrupted, don't be discouraged. Seek help from experienced writers or editors—they can offer valuable insights and strategies to get you back on track.

Writing doesn't truly begin with typing. It starts in the planning phase, with brainstorming, note-taking, and thoughtful organization. The act of creating something out of nothing—from characters to plotlines, or from hypotheses to conclusions—is a fundamental challenge of authorship. Yet, it is one you can overcome with perseverance, creativity, and a well-structured plan.

CHAPTER 2

Editing and Revising Your Work

The path to becoming a skilled writer often involves hard work and persistence, particularly when it comes to rewriting. The ability to revise effectively is an acquired skill, and its value cannot be overstated. However, it is crucial to strike a balance—over-polishing your draft can be as counterproductive as settling for mediocrity in your initial version. With the principle that "the best is the enemy of the good" in mind, having clear guidelines can help you achieve the right level of refinement.

One common pitfall in writing is verbosity, especially when the most important points are buried toward the end of paragraphs. Readers naturally progress from sentence to sentence, but often the most powerful or nuanced ideas are delayed. The solution lies in prioritizing key ideas, bringing them to the forefront through thoughtful reordering of sentences and careful adjustments to length and structure. With practice, you can transform your prose into something that engages and delights the reader.

Revisions represent the iterative process by which writing is improved—becoming more convincing, informative, or enjoyable. Each critique, digestion of feedback, and subsequent rewrite enhances the quality of the work. For experienced authors, this process is second nature, learned through trial and error. Writing a book, however, introduces unique challenges due to its sheer scale.

A long manuscript will rarely emerge flawless in its first draft. Recognizing this is vital. The process of refinement unfolds in three stages: composing the initial draft, identifying imperfections through a focused reading, and refining those flaws through rewrites. While the first two stages may feel more creative and enjoyable, the real heavy lifting occurs during revisions. It is this phase, albeit labor-intensive, that elevates a manuscript from adequate to exceptional.

The Importance of Editing

Authors often attempt to edit and proofread their work, but research shows that self-editing comes with significant limitations. Perceptual blindness—our tendency to see what we intended to write rather than what's actually on the page—combined with cognitive overload, makes it challenging to objectively review our own work. In long-form writing, such as novels or theses, it becomes even harder to identify structural issues or minor inconsistencies.

One effective approach is to set the manuscript aside for a few days to gain a fresh perspective. When returning to it, alternative methodologies, such as reading aloud or applying metrics like PlumX, can be useful for identifying overlooked errors. Collaborating with professional editors or research groups can also provide the external insight needed to refine your work. While some groups offer their services for free, others may require payment—but both options deliver significant benefits.

Editing is not merely a supplementary step in the writing process; it is foundational. While almost anyone can produce a first draft, it is through editing that a good text emerges. For academic and professional writing, editing and proofreading are indispensable for three main reasons:

1. **Logical Rigor and Cohesion**: Editors ensure the argument is coherent and well-organized, refining sentence structures to enhance clarity. They tailor your language for your target audience, ensuring it aligns with their knowledge level, expectations, and professional interests.
2. **Precision and Readability**: Editors maximize readability by favoring active voice, concise phrasing, and fluidity over unnecessary embellishments.
3. **Error Elimination**: From grammar and spelling to technical consistency in terms, abbreviations, and quotations, editors meticulously comb through your text to remove any mistakes.

An expertly edited manuscript achieves clarity, precision, and a logical flow that resonates with its audience. It ensures your ideas are communicated effectively, leaving a lasting impression on readers.

CHAPTER 3

Preparing for Publication

How do you know when your paper is ready for submission? This question lies at the heart of every author's journey. The simple answer is: *revision, revision, and more revision.* Before considering submission, it is essential to undertake multiple rounds of refinement to ensure your manuscript is polished and impactful.

A key step in this process is performing a **similarity check**. Reviewers are quick to identify excessive overlap between your manuscript and existing works, which often leads to rejection. Fortunately, there are many reliable software tools available, including **iThenticate, PlagScan, Turnitin,** and **Crossref Similarity Check**. These programs compare your text with vast networks of published content to assess originality. Many organizations and institutions also mandate that supervisors conduct similarity checks before internal reviews. While some authors may rely on colleagues for such evaluations, manual checks are far less reliable than using specialized software.

For me, the thrill of seeing a published paper never faded, but the path to acceptance was not without challenges. Like many authors, I received my fair share of rejection letters early in my career. These rejections were initially heartbreaking, but with time, I came to see them as part of the learning curve—a necessary step toward growth.

As an associate editor for two international soil science journals, I gained firsthand insight into the fairness and reasoning behind reviewers' critiques. What initially felt like harsh or unfair scores often had a solid basis, offering authors valuable lessons for improvement.

This chapter provides a comprehensive guide to the practical steps involved in preparing and submitting a manuscript. Recognizing the common difficulties faced during this phase, I have detailed every step, including technical challenges, and offered actionable solutions to make this journey less daunting.

Researching Publishing Options

Choosing the right publishing route is a pivotal decision that can shape the success and reach of your manuscript. Traditional publishers, for instance, often require authors to sell their rights in exchange for royalties—typically a small fraction of the purchase price. While these publishers offer benefits such as high print quality and favorable distribution policies, the road to securing a deal can be long, arduous, and discouraging.

For this reason, understanding the publishing process is essential to avoid common pitfalls. A **literary agent** can greatly enhance your manuscript's chances of success by providing an honest evaluation of your work, identifying niche audiences, offering professional advice, and expertly navigating the complexities of contracts and publisher negotiations.

Specialized publishers can also be a valuable option, particularly for works that involve multimedia components, online formats, or unique audience targeting. **Self-publishing** has become an increasingly popular route due to its affordability, flexibility, and speed. Main types of self-publishing include:

- **Electronic Pop-Up Books:** Ideal for creative, interactive formats.

- **Traditional Print-On-Demand (POD):** Offers professional quality without requiring large upfront investments.
- **Non-Traditional POD:** Targets niche markets or unconventional formats.

Among traditional publishers, there are various categories:

- **Large Trade Publishers:** Handle a majority of mainstream titles.
- **Academic Publishers:** Focus on scientific discoveries and professional achievements.
- **Educational Publishers:** Select content designed to support specific pedagogical goals.
- **Independent Publishers:** Cater to specialized or niche markets.
- **Custom Publishers:** Offer tailored solutions at any scale.

The first step in the publishing process is deciding on your publishing route. Factors to consider include:

1. **Audience**: Are you writing for scientific peers, a general readership, educators, or professionals?
2. **Goals**: Do you prioritize flexibility in presenting ideas, personal satisfaction, peer review, or speed?
3. **Profit and Reach**: What are your expectations regarding income and the size of your audience?
4. **Control**: How much influence do you want over the publication process?

For many, **self-publishing** via a personal website or POD service provides the fastest, most flexible, and often most cost-effective route. This approach allows authors to maintain creative control while reaching a wide audience.

CHAPTER 4

Navigating the Publishing Industry

Securing a literary agent can mark a pivotal turning point for any author. If an agent agrees to represent you, your manuscript bypasses the dreaded slush pile and moves several steps closer to publication. A skilled literary agent leverages their expertise and industry connections to negotiate better contracts, secure higher royalties, and garner more attention for your book. They can also help unlock opportunities for subsidiary sales, such as book clubs, foreign publishers, and specialty markets, broadening your work's reach and impact.

A good agent is more than just a business intermediary—they can become an invaluable partner in your career. The right agent will provide guidance across multiple aspects of the publishing process, from editorial decisions to marketing strategies. Before selecting an agent, it's wise to seek feedback from their current or past authors. Do they consistently support their clients' long-term goals? Are they effective in navigating the complexities of the publishing world? Choosing an agent who aligns with your vision and aspirations can make all the difference in your success.

While self-publishers rely on personal networks and their own efforts to market and distribute their work, literary agents and publishing house professionals often have the expertise to guide an author's career strategically. Ultimately, both paths—traditional and self-publishing—require careful consideration of your goals, resources, and the level of control you wish to maintain.

Publishing Options: A Modern Landscape

The publishing world today offers authors a diverse array of options, each with its own advantages and challenges. It's much like a choose-your-own-adventure story: the route you select depends on your objectives, resources, and preferences.

If you relish control over the details of your book's design, distribution, and marketing, then self-publishing could be the right path for you. Self-publishing allows you to implement creative marketing ideas, tailor products tied to your book, and directly engage with your audience. However, it also demands substantial commitment in terms of time, budget, and project management. You'll need to handle tasks ranging from coordinating print runs to running ad campaigns on platforms like Amazon.

On the other hand, if your book is particularly important, groundbreaking, or uniquely captivating, you might prefer to submit it to a traditional publisher rather than risk it languishing in obscurity. Traditional publishers often provide the resources and reach needed to make such works shine.

Regardless of the path you choose, it's essential to evaluate the timeline for publication, your available free time, and your ability to manage sequential tasks. These considerations will help guide your decision, ensuring that your chosen approach aligns with your goals and lifestyle.

Traditional vs. Self-Publishing

When choosing between traditional and self-publishing, lifestyle factors play a crucial role. Both options require authors to promote their work, but the nature of that promotion varies. Traditional publishing often demands attendance at events, signings, and book fairs, particularly during the later stages of the publishing process. While this can involve extensive travel, traditional publishers may also offer logistical support, reducing the strain on authors.

In contrast, self-publishing places greater emphasis on digital presence. Self-published authors often maintain active blogs, websites, and social media profiles while investing in targeted advertising campaigns through platforms like Amazon. This level of involvement requires a willingness to take charge of every aspect of the book's promotion and distribution.

Fortunately, both paths are now widely recognized as valid and legitimate. A decade ago, self-publishing was stigmatized, seen as a last resort for writers unable to secure traditional deals. However, advancements in technology and changing consumer preferences have transformed indie publishing into a powerful and respected option. Many authors now use self-publishing as a springboard, gaining visibility and credibility that may eventually attract traditional publishers.

This decision ultimately depends on your priorities: Is creative control your top concern? Are you aiming for speed and affordability? Or do you seek the prestige and professional support that come with traditional publishing? By seeking advice, conducting thorough research, and reflecting on your goals, you can make an informed choice that aligns with your vision for your book.

CHAPTER 5

Building Your Author Platform

In today's publishing world, success no longer hinges solely on the quality of your writing—it also depends on your ability to market your work. Publishing has evolved into a marketing-driven process, and as an author, you must embrace this shift. While some authors are fortunate enough to have a dedicated social media consultant at their publisher, many must take the reins themselves, particularly when it comes to building an online presence.

Consider this example: one professional author we know keeps digital photographs of his book covers readily available on his computer. At readings and signings, he sets up his computer for audience engagement. Before signing books, he uploads a photo of each personalized autograph to his Facebook account, typing a personal message for every follower. These posts not only create a sense of connection with his audience but also boost his online visibility.

Similarly, bestselling author Jenni Holm and her husband, graphic novelist Matthew Holm, have mastered the art of leveraging school visits to build their online platform. By engaging directly with students and inviting them to follow their Facebook page, they often gain hundreds, if not thousands, of new connections overnight. This tangible proof of audience engagement strengthens their relationship with their publishers and demonstrates their marketing impact.

Congratulations—whether you've published your first book or are an established name with multiple titles, you now have the opportunity to present yourself as an author with a strong and supportive platform. The internet offers you an unlimited array of marketing tools, and with a strategic approach, you can elevate your publishing efforts to new heights.

Utilizing Social Media

Social media has become an essential tool for authors to promote their work, connect with audiences, and increase the visibility of their publications. Nearly all major publishers and journals have active social media accounts, which they use to share links to newly published articles and books. By tagging authors and engaging with their audiences, publishers amplify the reach of your work across networks.

As an author, you can take inspiration from this approach. Following the official social media accounts of publishers, journals, and relevant literary organizations allows you to stay informed about industry trends while also positioning yourself within the broader conversation.

Video content, in particular, has emerged as a highly effective medium for engagement. Studies indicate that 72% of individuals prefer video over other forms of content, whether on social media platforms, websites, or embedded within articles. Creating and sharing short, visually engaging videos about your book—such as behind-the-scenes insights, reading excerpts, or interviews—can captivate your audience and drive interest in your work.

Today, the range of social media platforms available is vast. Popular options like Facebook, Twitter, LinkedIn, and YouTube remain powerful tools for audience engagement. For more academic or research-focused authors, platforms like ResearchGate, Mendeley, and Academia.edu provide opportunities to share work within specialized communities.

By using social media effectively, authors can foster meaningful two-way communication with their audience. Sharing your work through these platforms not only increases its visibility but also establishes you as an active participant in the literary or scholarly community. With consistency, creativity, and proper strategy, social media can become one of the most powerful assets in building your author platform.

CHAPTER 6

Marketing and Promoting Your Book

Marketing your book begins long before the final chapter is written. Identifying your potential audience and determining how to reach them is the foundation of your promotional strategy. Start by building an online presence—consider launching a blog, Facebook page, or Twitter account dedicated to your book. Use these platforms to share interesting facts, progress updates, and even behind-the-scenes glimpses, such as pictures of your characters or setting inspirations. Tease future developments and create a sense of anticipation, encouraging readers to engage with your narrative even before publication.

Craft a tagline or description that encapsulates your book's essence and appeals to your target audience. This will serve as the cornerstone of your publishing brand, making your work memorable and easily identifiable. Stay connected with your readers through regular updates, exclusive sneak peeks, and exciting news, gradually fostering a sense of community around your book. Concurrently, research potential reviewers and publications that align with your book's theme or genre. Building a network of reviewers and promotional outlets can greatly enhance visibility and credibility.

While traditional publishers do contribute to promotional efforts, their budgets are often constrained, and authors are increasingly expected to share the marketing burden. Many independent companies offer specialized marketing packages for self-published authors, though these can be cost-prohibitive. Regardless of your publishing route, your efforts as an author can significantly amplify your book's reach and impact.

Book Launch Strategies

The journey of self-publishing has become the go-to path for many modern authors. Regardless of whether you choose self-publishing or traditional publishing, having a solid plan for your book's launch is essential. Engaging in online forums or writer communities, where authors share their daily progress—such as "Today I wrote 2 pages. Goodnight!"—can help sustain motivation and foster creativity. As Hermann Hesse insightfully remarked, "Each book is hidden in another book." By embracing a positive and collaborative mindset, authors can unlock hidden depths in their own work while drawing inspiration from others.

Launching a book is a memorable milestone for any author. The months spent crafting the manuscript are only the prelude to the labor-intensive phase of promotion and marketing. However, the journey need not be a solitary one. Collaborating with other authors, friends, and family can bring fresh ideas and support to your efforts. Sharing your favorite passages with acquaintances or even strangers can be immensely gratifying and may spark meaningful connections.

Book launches offer the opportunity to build relationships not just with readers, but also with fellow authors. These connections can inspire younger writers, reminding them that their own "someday I'll write a book" can become a reality with dedication and perseverance. On the road to publication, every "today" is a crucial step toward that dream.

CHAPTER 7

Engaging with Readers

For many authors, publishing a literary work is only the first step—it doesn't always directly equate to success. Some writers or researchers may not feel the desire to actively promote their work, let alone strategize how to do so. This is particularly true in academia, where juggling the demands of research, writing, and teaching can make marketing seem like a luxury rather than a priority. However, engaging with readers—both potential and existing—can be transformative, elevating an author's career, creating meaningful connections, and fostering valuable feedback.

Not every outreach channel works for every author, and that's okay. Success lies in identifying the platforms and methods that align with your strengths and audience. Scholarly authors, for instance, often find their work utilized by a range of individuals—students, translators, editors, and academics. Engaging with these readers can pave the way for collaboration, inspiration, and even greater visibility.

Authors have a variety of ways to connect with readers. After publication, reading reviews and responding to feedback can offer insights and help strengthen your relationship with your audience. Beyond that, remaining active throughout the publishing process—before, during, and after the release—can keep your work fresh in the minds of readers.

Social media platforms are among the most effective tools for engagement. Many authors use Twitter, Facebook, LinkedIn, or Instagram to share ideas, updates, book campaigns, and links to publications. While follower numbers vary, what truly matters is how an author makes use of these connections. Blogging is another excellent avenue, enabling authors to share insights, academic expertise, and research findings with a broader audience. Whether it's through a tweet, post, or blog entry, engaging with readers demonstrates that your work is more than words on a page—it's part of an ongoing conversation.

Building a Fanbase

A loyal fanbase is a treasure for any author, especially those who write speculative nonfiction or consistently explore a particular topic. Readers who resonate with your work are not easily found, and their support should never be taken for granted. You've worked hard to cultivate an audience, so it's essential to keep them informed and engaged.

For your readers, your book isn't just a product—it's a shared experience. They invest in your words, ideas, and perspective, making it just as important to them as it is to you. Let them know about your progress, upcoming projects, and plans. Whether through emails, social media updates, or even traditional business cards, maintaining communication keeps your audience connected to your journey.

Building a fanbase takes time and consistent effort, but it's a worthwhile investment. Publishers, even the most successful ones, rarely have dedicated staff to promote individual books. Much of the work of building awareness falls on the author's shoulders. By actively cultivating a fanbase, you ensure that your audience knows who you are, what you're creating, and why they should be excited about your work.

As your book begins to take shape, think about the kind of audience you want to reach. Who are they? What are their interests? Once you've identified your target readers, you can tailor your approach to connect with them effectively. Keep in mind that the process of building a fanbase doesn't end with the book launch—it's an ongoing commitment to fostering relationships and sharing your creative journey.

CHAPTER 8

Copyright and Legal Considerations

When publishing with IGI Global, contributors are required to complete an electronic Contributor Information (CI) Form. This form serves multiple purposes, helping IGI Global manage workflow-related initiatives, such as identifying book preferences, specifying index terms, and linking content to appropriate databases. The hard copy of the contributor form is no longer necessary or accepted, as electronic submissions streamline processes and safeguard against potential loss.

Rest assured, all information provided in this form is used exclusively for metadata and reference purposes, ensuring a smooth publishing process. By submitting the CI Form during the content-submission stage, authors help accelerate the indexing process, which occurs after the final submission. This step ensures that your work is properly cataloged and easily discoverable through global indexes and databases.

Authors publishing with IGI Global also have the option to sign an **exclusive license agreement**. This agreement grants the publisher specific rights to use and distribute the work, while offering authors the opportunity to submit their chapters to various indexes for increased accessibility and visibility. The IGI Global Copyright Agreement Form also assures that the manuscript is original, unpublished, and not under consideration elsewhere. Authors seeking more details about relevant journals or books can explore the **IGI Global Indexing and Abstracting Coverage webpage** for additional resources.

Protecting Your Intellectual Property

Protecting your intellectual property (IP) ensures your work reaches the audience it deserves while safeguarding your rights as its creator. If you are preparing to distribute a working paper on the World Wide Web, here's a helpful guide:

1. **Prepare a PDF:** Create a portable document file (PDF) of the full paper, and include a footnote on the title page with the current date. Use a clear and legible font, such as 11-point Helvetica, to enhance readability.
2. **University Distribution:** If presenting your paper at a university, save a dated copy of the paper onto a labeled disk, noting your name, department, paper title, and contact information. Consider uploading the paper to the university's FTP for distribution.
3. **Seek Permissions:** Before sharing earlier versions of your paper, secure written permissions to reuse content as required by publishers or journals. For example, copyright release forms should permit Web distribution and submission to platforms like SSRN or Elsevier.

For authors publishing with Elsevier, their policy allows working-paper versions to remain on the Web, provided the final proof includes a notice specifying that the published version is for educational use only.

Taking additional measures to safeguard your work can reduce the risk of unauthorized use. For instance:

- **File Formats:** Scanning your papers in non-text-readable .tiff format discourages unauthorized reformatting. Similarly, using .ccx graphic files offers high resolution and resists easy modification.
- **Version Tracking:** Maintain records of where and when each version of your work is distributed. Citing working-paper versions can also deter others from duplicating your material.

Investing time in protecting your IP not only preserves your rights but also promotes your work effectively, enabling it to reach a wider audience while ensuring proper attribution.

CHAPTER 9

Achieving Success as an Author

Success in authorship often transcends the immediate rewards of publication or financial gain. According to Garreau, the devotion one invests in their craft—the time and energy dedicated to creating something meaningful—can lead to a legacy that outlasts their lifetime. Interestingly, some of the most successful artists are not driven by greed or a hunger for power. Instead, they follow their passions, prioritizing artistic integrity over fleeting trends or short-term recognition.

McLaurin and Dorsey echo this sentiment, defining true success as "writing to the best of your ability." It is about infusing discipline and artistry into your work to the fullest extent that your talent allows. This commitment requires perseverance in the face of challenges, an ability to discuss and share your work confidently, and the patience to endure the slower, sometimes less glamorous aspects of the author's journey—like long book-signing events or repeated revisions.

So, how does an author achieve artistic success? While the definition varies, some key characteristics stand out. Success can mean seeing your words in print or digital form, gaining recognition through positive reviews, or earning a lasting reputation among critics and readers. However, great authors often measure their success differently—they strive to uphold timeless aesthetics, ethical principles, and a deeper moral resonance in their work.

This chapter explores the concept of success, highlights criteria that contribute to it, and provides examples of notable individuals and works that embody artistic achievement. By embracing a thoughtful and disciplined approach, authors can pursue success that aligns with their values and leaves a lasting impact.

Setting Realistic Goals

Achieving success begins with setting clear, actionable goals. A well-defined goal serves as a roadmap, guiding you toward higher aspirations—whether that's escaping academia, becoming a sought-after expert, establishing a renowned research lab, or attaining a prominent leadership position. The more specific your goals are, the more attainable they become. Specificity helps you identify the steps required to achieve them, determine necessary resources, and plan your timeline effectively.

For example, instead of aiming to "write the best book ever," break the process into tangible milestones, such as completing a chapter draft within a set timeframe or researching a specific aspect of your topic. Regularly revisiting and updating your goals keeps you accountable and motivated.

It's important to aim high—ambitious goals often lead to greater achievements, even if you fall short. However, goals should also remain attainable, relevant, and tied to clear deadlines. This brings us to the SMART framework for goal-setting:

- **Specific**: Define your goal in precise terms.
- **Measurable**: Track your progress with clear metrics.
- **Attainable**: Ensure the goal is challenging yet realistic.

- **Relevant**: Focus on objectives that align with your broader ambitions.
- **Time-bound**: Set a deadline to maintain momentum.

For example, if you conduct four experiments a year and believe each could lead to a manuscript, you might set a production goal of completing one manuscript every three months. Aligning your goals with your workload and available time ensures they remain practical and achievable.

By setting SMART goals, you create a structured pathway to success, allowing you to maintain focus and track your progress. Success as an author may take many forms, but with dedication, discipline, and clear objectives, you can steadily work toward realizing your vision.

Conclusion and Next Steps

We understand the content and its potential applications. This book is designed to be a valuable, practical, and relevant resource for authors at all stages of their careers. Whether you're a student, an early-career researcher, an established scholar, a supervisor coaching students toward publication, or even a reviewer or tutor, this guide offers tools and strategies that adapt to your needs.

Each of these groups will use the guide in unique ways. For students, it demystifies the writing and publishing process, empowering them to create work that meets academic standards. For supervisors and tutors, it provides insights to help their mentees succeed. Reviewers may find the advice helpful for evaluating submissions, while established researchers can use the guide to refine their craft further.

The timing of this book aligns with the current academic landscape. The pressure to publish is greater than ever, with a growing number of students pursuing advanced degrees and funding bodies increasingly expecting tangible outputs from research projects. While journals continue to proliferate, the number of submissions has risen exponentially in many fields. As authors, we must ask ourselves two critical questions: *Who will read this?* and *Why does the world need another journal article on this topic?* If we can't answer these questions honestly, we should revisit our work with fresh purpose and focus.

We hope this guide will inspire you to tackle these essential challenges with enthusiasm and curiosity. Good luck as you embark on your writing journey!

Continuing Your Writing Journey

Every book idea starts with a spark—an intriguing topic that lingers in your thoughts and grows into a vision. The real challenge, however, lies not in having the idea but in believing that you can turn it into a book. The ideal topic is neither so shallow that it cannot sustain an entire manuscript nor so personal that it fails to engage a broader audience.

If you've reached the conclusion that your idea is viable, the next steps involve thorough research and the courage to translate your thoughts into words. Writing a book demands more than technical skill—it requires passion, dedication, and the confidence to share your unique perspective with the world. As Bernard Shaw aptly said, "If you've got the fire, let it burn."

Writing a book is not for the faint-hearted—it's a far more challenging endeavor than crafting an article or shorter piece. However, it also offers unparalleled rewards. A well-executed book can elevate your profile as a writer, establish you as an authority in your field, and reinvigorate your career. It showcases your ability to not only generate ideas but also to research, organize, and present them in a way that adds value to your audience.

If you feel ready to undertake this journey, what comes next? This book has equipped you with strategies and advice to tackle the process with confidence. If you possess the special knowledge, professional expertise, and determination required to write a book, now is the time to act. Remember, writing is not just about creating a product—it's about contributing meaningfully to the world.

As you move forward, keep this guide close at hand. Let it serve as both a resource and a reminder that great writing is within your reach. Good luck, and may your passion for writing lead you to new and exciting opportunities!

www.ingramcontent.com/pod-product-compliance
Lightning Source LLC
LaVergne TN
LVHW092102060526
838201LV00047B/1521